This

GRATITUDE

Journal

BELONGS TO

_____

_____

_____

_____

Things I love
about my life

Date: _____

The activities that make me happy:

_____

_____

_____

_____

_____

I will try to do them more often by:

_____

_____

_____

_____

_____

Movies

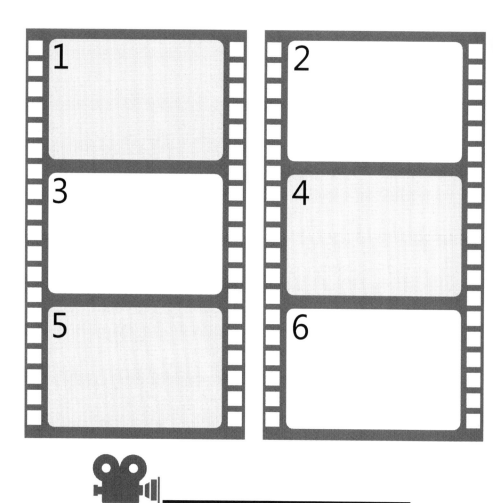

I AM GRATEFUL FOR:

1

2

3

4

5

6

GRATITUDE
Prompts

1. WHO DO YOU LOVE?
2. WHAT MADE YOU SMILE LATELY?
3. WHO DO YOU LIKE?
4. WHAT ARE YOU GOOD AT DOING?
5. WHO CAN YOU COUNT ON?
6. WHAT DO YOU LOVE?
7. WHAT DO YOU LIKE?
8. WHERE DO YOU LIKE TO GO?
9. WHAT DO YOU ENJOY?
10. WHO INSPIRES YOU?
11. LIST ACTIVITIES THAT BRING YOU JOY.
12. LIST ITEMS THAT BRING YOU JOY.
13. LIST PEOPLE THAT BRING YOU JOY.
14. WHAT MAKES YOU HAPPY?
15. WHAT RELAXES YOU?
16. WHAT MAKES YOU SPECIAL?
17. WHAT IS YOUR FAVORITE MEMORY?
18. IS THERE ANYTHING THAT YOU TAKE FOR GRANTED?
19. WHAT IS YOUR FAVORITE FOOD?
20. DESCRIBE ONE GOOD THING THAT
HAPPENED TO YOU THIS MONTH.

PLACES

I enjoyed visiting:

_____

_____

_____

_____

_____

_____

PEOPLE

I am Grateful For:

_____

_____

_____

_____

_____

_____

_____

_____

GRATEFUL FOR

Monday:

Tuesday:

Wednesday:

Thursday:

Friday:

Saturday:

Sunday:

Thank You

Dear
_____
_____
_____
_____
_____
_____
_____
_____

_____

_____

_____

You don't actually have to send the letter

Things I love
about my life

Date: _____

The activities that make me happy:

_____

_____

_____

_____

_____

I will try to do them more often by:

_____

_____

_____

_____

_____

Movies

I AM GRATEFUL FOR:

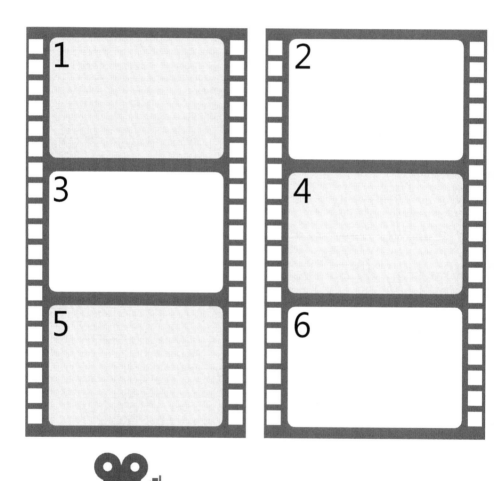

1

2

3

4

5

6

GRATITUDE

Prompts

1. WHO DO YOU LOVE?
2. WHAT MADE YOU SMILE LATELY?
3. WHO DO YOU LIKE?
4. WHAT ARE YOU GOOD AT DOING?
5. WHO CAN YOU COUNT ON?
6. WHAT DO YOU LOVE?
7. WHAT DO YOU LIKE?
8. WHERE DO YOU LIKE TO GO?
9. WHAT DO YOU ENJOY?
10. WHO INSPIRES YOU?
11. LIST ACTIVITIES THAT BRING YOU JOY.
12. LIST ITEMS THAT BRING YOU JOY.
13. LIST PEOPLE THAT BRING YOU JOY.
14. WHAT MAKES YOU HAPPY?
15. WHAT RELAXES YOU?
16. WHAT MAKES YOU SPECIAL?
17. WHAT IS YOUR FAVORITE MEMORY?
18. IS THERE ANYTHING THAT YOU TAKE FOR GRANTED?
19. WHAT IS YOUR FAVORITE FOOD?
20. DESCRIBE ONE GOOD THING THAT
HAPPENED TO YOU THIS MONTH.

PLACES

I enjoyed visiting:

📍 _____

📍 _____

📍 _____

📍 _____

📍 _____

📍 _____

PEOPLE

I am Grateful For:

_____

_____

_____

_____

_____

_____

_____

_____

GRATEFUL FOR

Monday:

Tuesday:

Wednesday:

Thursday:

Friday:

Saturday:

Sunday:

Thank You

Dear

_____
_____
_____
_____
_____
_____
_____
_____
_____
_____

You don't actually have to send the letter

Things I love
about my life

Date: _____

The activities that make me happy:

_____

_____

_____

_____

_____

I will try to do them more often by:

_____

_____

_____

_____

_____

Movies

I AM GRATEFUL FOR:

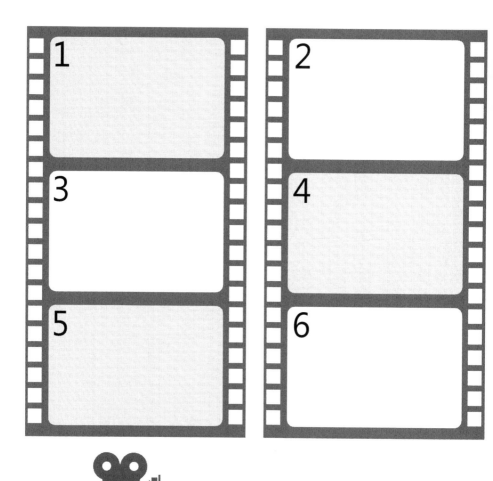

1

2

3

4

5

6

GRATITUDE
Prompts

1. WHO DO YOU LOVE?
2. WHAT MADE YOU SMILE LATELY?
3. WHO DO YOU LIKE?
4. WHAT ARE YOU GOOD AT DOING?
5. WHO CAN YOU COUNT ON?
6. WHAT DO YOU LOVE?
7. WHAT DO YOU LIKE?
8. WHERE DO YOU LIKE TO GO?
9. WHAT DO YOU ENJOY?
10. WHO INSPIRES YOU?
11. LIST ACTIVITIES THAT BRING YOU JOY.
12. LIST ITEMS THAT BRING YOU JOY.
13. LIST PEOPLE THAT BRING YOU JOY.
14. WHAT MAKES YOU HAPPY?
15. WHAT RELAXES YOU?
16. WHAT MAKES YOU SPECIAL?
17. WHAT IS YOUR FAVORITE MEMORY?
18. IS THERE ANYTHING THAT YOU TAKE FOR GRANTED?
19. WHAT IS YOUR FAVORITE FOOD?
20. DESCRIBE ONE GOOD THING THAT
HAPPENED TO YOU THIS MONTH.

PLACES

I enjoyed visiting:

📍 _____

📍 _____

📍 _____

📍 _____

📍 _____

📍 _____

PEOPLE

I am Grateful For:

_____

_____

_____

_____

_____

_____

_____

_____

GRATEFUL FOR

Monday:

Tuesday:

Wednesday:

Thursday:

Friday:

Saturday:

Sunday:

Thank You

Dear

_____

_____

_____

_____

_____

_____

_____

_____

_____

_____

_____

You don't actually have to send the letter

Things I love
about my life

Date: _____

The activities that make me happy:

_____

_____

_____

_____

_____

I will try to do them more often by:

_____

_____

_____

_____

_____

Movies

I AM GRATEFUL FOR:

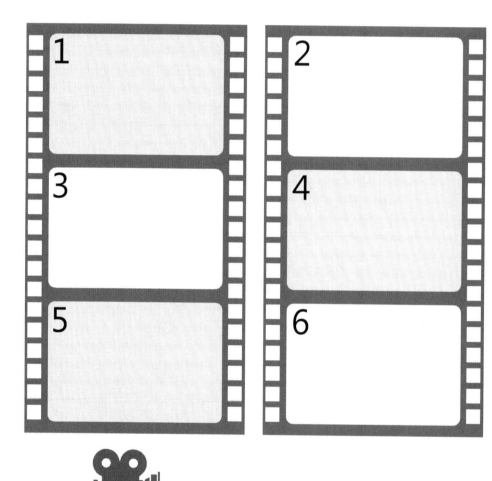

1

2

3

4

5

6

GRATITUDE
Prompts

1. WHO DO YOU LOVE?
2. WHAT MADE YOU SMILE LATELY?
3. WHO DO YOU LIKE?
4. WHAT ARE YOU GOOD AT DOING?
5. WHO CAN YOU COUNT ON?
6. WHAT DO YOU LOVE?
7. WHAT DO YOU LIKE?
8. WHERE DO YOU LIKE TO GO?
9. WHAT DO YOU ENJOY?
10. WHO INSPIRES YOU?
11. LIST ACTIVITIES THAT BRING YOU JOY.
12. LIST ITEMS THAT BRING YOU JOY.
13. LIST PEOPLE THAT BRING YOU JOY.
14. WHAT MAKES YOU HAPPY?
15. WHAT RELAXES YOU?
16. WHAT MAKES YOU SPECIAL?
17. WHAT IS YOUR FAVORITE MEMORY?
18. IS THERE ANYTHING THAT YOU TAKE FOR GRANTED?
19. WHAT IS YOUR FAVORITE FOOD?
20. DESCRIBE ONE GOOD THING THAT
HAPPENED TO YOU THIS MONTH.

PLACES

I enjoyed visiting:

_____

_____

_____

_____

_____

_____

PEOPLE

I am Grateful For:

_____

_____

_____

_____

_____

_____

_____

GRATEFUL FOR

Monday:

Tuesday:

Wednesday:

Thursday:

Friday:

Saturday:

Sunday:

Thank You

Dear

You don't actually have to send the letter

Things I love
about my life

Date: _____

The activities that make me happy:

_____

_____

_____

_____

_____

I will try to do them more often by:

_____

_____

_____

_____

_____

Movies

I AM GRATEFUL FOR:

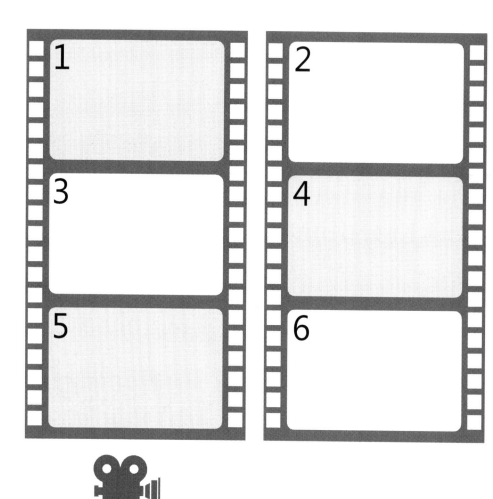

1

2

3

4

5

6

GRATITUDE
Prompts

1. WHO DO YOU LOVE?
2. WHAT MADE YOU SMILE LATELY?
3. WHO DO YOU LIKE?
4. WHAT ARE YOU GOOD AT DOING?
5. WHO CAN YOU COUNT ON?
6. WHAT DO YOU LOVE?
7. WHAT DO YOU LIKE?
8. WHERE DO YOU LIKE TO GO?
9. WHAT DO YOU ENJOY?
10. WHO INSPIRES YOU?
11. LIST ACTIVITIES THAT BRING YOU JOY.
12. LIST ITEMS THAT BRING YOU JOY.
13. LIST PEOPLE THAT BRING YOU JOY.
14. WHAT MAKES YOU HAPPY?
15. WHAT RELAXES YOU?
16. WHAT MAKES YOU SPECIAL?
17. WHAT IS YOUR FAVORITE MEMORY?
18. IS THERE ANYTHING THAT YOU TAKE FOR GRANTED?
19. WHAT IS YOUR FAVORITE FOOD?
20. DESCRIBE ONE GOOD THING THAT
HAPPENED TO YOU THIS MONTH.

PLACES

I enjoyed visiting:

_____

_____

_____

_____

_____

_____

PEOPLE

I am Grateful For:

_____

_____

_____

_____

_____

_____

_____

GRATEFUL FOR

Monday:

Tuesday:

Wednesday:

Thursday:

Friday:

Saturday:

Sunday:

Thank You

Dear

_____
_____
_____
_____
_____
_____
_____
_____
_____

_____
_____

You don't actually have to send the letter

Things I love
about my life

Date: _____

The activities that make me happy:

_____

_____

_____

_____

_____

I will try to do them more often by:

_____

_____

_____

_____

_____

Movies

I AM GRATEFUL FOR:

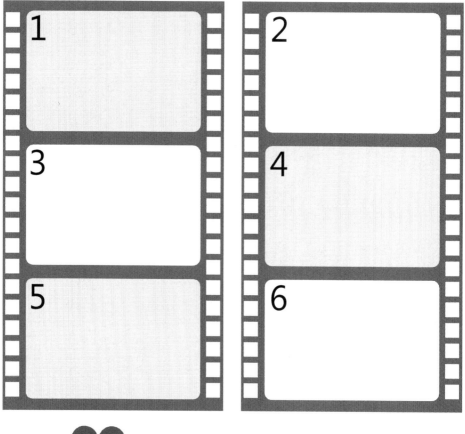

1

2

3

4

5

6

GRATITUDE
Prompts

1. WHO DO YOU LOVE?
2. WHAT MADE YOU SMILE LATELY?
3. WHO DO YOU LIKE?
4. WHAT ARE YOU GOOD AT DOING?
5. WHO CAN YOU COUNT ON?
6. WHAT DO YOU LOVE?
7. WHAT DO YOU LIKE?
8. WHERE DO YOU LIKE TO GO?
9. WHAT DO YOU ENJOY?
10. WHO INSPIRES YOU?
11. LIST ACTIVITIES THAT BRING YOU JOY.
12. LIST ITEMS THAT BRING YOU JOY.
13. LIST PEOPLE THAT BRING YOU JOY.
14. WHAT MAKES YOU HAPPY?
15. WHAT RELAXES YOU?
16. WHAT MAKES YOU SPECIAL?
17. WHAT IS YOUR FAVORITE MEMORY?
18. IS THERE ANYTHING THAT YOU TAKE FOR GRANTED?
19. WHAT IS YOUR FAVORITE FOOD?
20. DESCRIBE ONE GOOD THING THAT
HAPPENED TO YOU THIS MONTH.

PLACES

I enjoyed visiting:

PEOPLE

I am Grateful For:

_____

_____

_____

_____

_____

_____

_____

_____

GRATEFUL FOR

Monday:

Tuesday:

Wednesday:

Thursday:

Friday:

Saturday:

Sunday:

Thank You

Dear
_____
_____
_____
_____
_____
_____
_____
_____

_____

_____

_____

You don't actually have to send the letter

Things I love
about my life

Date: _____

The activities that make me happy:

_____

_____

_____

_____

_____

I will try to do them more often by:

_____

_____

_____

_____

_____

Movies

I AM GRATEFUL FOR:

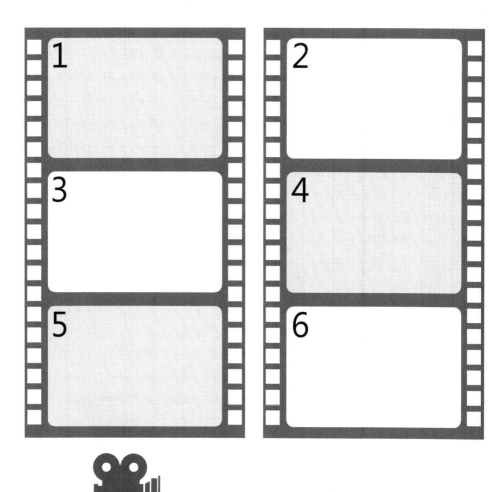

1

2

3

4

5

6

GRATITUDE
Prompts

1. WHO DO YOU LOVE?
2. WHAT MADE YOU SMILE LATELY?
3. WHO DO YOU LIKE?
4. WHAT ARE YOU GOOD AT DOING?
5. WHO CAN YOU COUNT ON?
6. WHAT DO YOU LOVE?
7. WHAT DO YOU LIKE?
8. WHERE DO YOU LIKE TO GO?
9. WHAT DO YOU ENJOY?
10. WHO INSPIRES YOU?
11. LIST ACTIVITIES THAT BRING YOU JOY.
12. LIST ITEMS THAT BRING YOU JOY.
13. LIST PEOPLE THAT BRING YOU JOY.
14. WHAT MAKES YOU HAPPY?
15. WHAT RELAXES YOU?
16. WHAT MAKES YOU SPECIAL?
17. WHAT IS YOUR FAVORITE MEMORY?
18. IS THERE ANYTHING THAT YOU TAKE FOR GRANTED?
19. WHAT IS YOUR FAVORITE FOOD?
20. DESCRIBE ONE GOOD THING THAT
HAPPENED TO YOU THIS MONTH.

PLACES

I enjoyed visiting:

_____

_____

_____

_____

_____

_____

PEOPLE

I am Grateful For:

_____

_____

_____

_____

_____

_____

_____

GRATEFUL FOR

Monday:

Tuesday:

Wednesday:

Thursday:

Friday:

Saturday:

Sunday:

Thank You

Dear _____

_____

_____

_____

_____

_____

_____

_____

_____

_____

_____

You don't actually have to send the letter

Things I love about my life

Date: _____

The activities that make me happy:

_____

_____

_____

_____

_____

I will try to do them more often by:

_____

_____

_____

_____

_____

Movies

I AM GRATEFUL FOR:

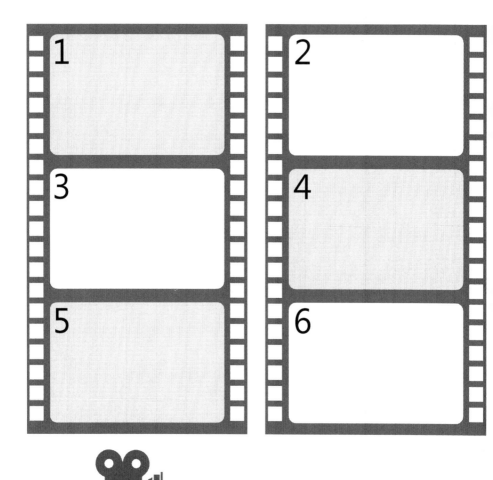

1

2

3

4

5

6

GRATITUDE
Prompts

1. WHO DO YOU LOVE?
2. WHAT MADE YOU SMILE LATELY?
3. WHO DO YOU LIKE?
4. WHAT ARE YOU GOOD AT DOING?
5. WHO CAN YOU COUNT ON?
6. WHAT DO YOU LOVE?
7. WHAT DO YOU LIKE?
8. WHERE DO YOU LIKE TO GO?
9. WHAT DO YOU ENJOY?
10. WHO INSPIRES YOU?
11. LIST ACTIVITIES THAT BRING YOU JOY.
12. LIST ITEMS THAT BRING YOU JOY.
13. LIST PEOPLE THAT BRING YOU JOY.
14. WHAT MAKES YOU HAPPY?
15. WHAT RELAXES YOU?
16. WHAT MAKES YOU SPECIAL?
17. WHAT IS YOUR FAVORITE MEMORY?
18. IS THERE ANYTHING THAT YOU TAKE FOR GRANTED?
19. WHAT IS YOUR FAVORITE FOOD?
20. DESCRIBE ONE GOOD THING THAT
HAPPENED TO YOU THIS MONTH.

PLACES

I enjoyed visiting:

📍 _____

📍 _____

📍 _____

📍 _____

📍 _____

📍 _____

PEOPLE

I am Grateful For:

_____

_____

_____

_____

_____

_____

_____

GRATEFUL FOR

Monday:

Tuesday:

Wednesday:

Thursday:

Friday:

Saturday:

Sunday:

Thank You

Dear

You don't actually have to send the letter

Things I love
about my life

Date: _____

_____

_____

_____

_____

_____

_____

_____

_____

_____

_____

_____

_____

_____

The activities that make me happy:

_____

_____

_____

_____

_____

I will try to do them more often by:

_____

_____

_____

_____

_____

Movies

I AM GRATEFUL FOR:

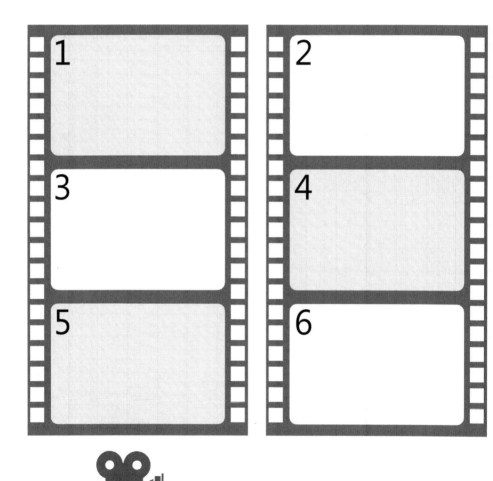

1

2

3

4

5

6

GRATITUDE
Prompts

1. WHO DO YOU LOVE?
2. WHAT MADE YOU SMILE LATELY?
3. WHO DO YOU LIKE?
4. WHAT ARE YOU GOOD AT DOING?
5. WHO CAN YOU COUNT ON?
6. WHAT DO YOU LOVE?
7. WHAT DO YOU LIKE?
8. WHERE DO YOU LIKE TO GO?
9. WHAT DO YOU ENJOY?
10. WHO INSPIRES YOU?
11. LIST ACTIVITIES THAT BRING YOU JOY.
12. LIST ITEMS THAT BRING YOU JOY.
13. LIST PEOPLE THAT BRING YOU JOY.
14. WHAT MAKES YOU HAPPY?
15. WHAT RELAXES YOU?
16. WHAT MAKES YOU SPECIAL?
17. WHAT IS YOUR FAVORITE MEMORY?
18. IS THERE ANYTHING THAT YOU TAKE FOR GRANTED?
19. WHAT IS YOUR FAVORITE FOOD?
20. DESCRIBE ONE GOOD THING THAT
HAPPENED TO YOU THIS MONTH.

PLACES

I enjoyed visiting:

_____

_____

_____

_____

_____

_____

PEOPLE

I am Grateful For:

_____

_____

_____

_____

_____

_____

_____

GRATEFUL FOR

Monday:

Tuesday:

Wednesday:

Thursday:

Friday:

Saturday:

Sunday:

Thank You

Dear

_____

_____

_____

_____

_____

_____

_____

_____

_____

_____

_____

_____

You don't actually have to send the letter

Things I love
about my life

Date: _____

The activities that make me happy:

_____

_____

_____

_____

_____

I will try to do them more often by:

_____

_____

_____

_____

_____

Movies

I AM GRATEFUL FOR:

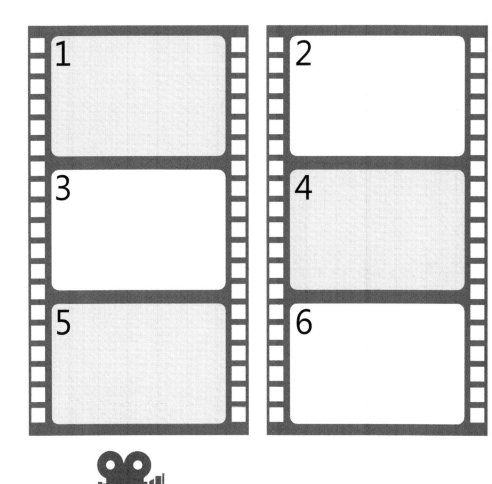

1

2

3

4

5

6

GRATITUDE
Prompts

1. WHO DO YOU LOVE?
2. WHAT MADE YOU SMILE LATELY?
3. WHO DO YOU LIKE?
4. WHAT ARE YOU GOOD AT DOING?
5. WHO CAN YOU COUNT ON?
6. WHAT DO YOU LOVE?
7. WHAT DO YOU LIKE?
8. WHERE DO YOU LIKE TO GO?
9. WHAT DO YOU ENJOY?
10. WHO INSPIRES YOU?
11. LIST ACTIVITIES THAT BRING YOU JOY.
12. LIST ITEMS THAT BRING YOU JOY.
13. LIST PEOPLE THAT BRING YOU JOY.
14. WHAT MAKES YOU HAPPY?
15. WHAT RELAXES YOU?
16. WHAT MAKES YOU SPECIAL?
17. WHAT IS YOUR FAVORITE MEMORY?
18. IS THERE ANYTHING THAT YOU TAKE FOR GRANTED?
19. WHAT IS YOUR FAVORITE FOOD?
20. DESCRIBE ONE GOOD THING THAT
 HAPPENED TO YOU THIS MONTH.

PLACES

I enjoyed visiting:

_____

_____

_____

_____

_____

_____

PEOPLE

I am Grateful For:

_____

_____

_____

_____

_____

_____

_____

GRATEFUL FOR

Monday:

Tuesday:

Wednesday:

Thursday:

Friday:

Saturday:

Sunday:

Thank You

Dear
_____
_____
_____
_____
_____
_____
_____
_____
_____
_____

_____

_____

____

You don't actually have to send the letter

Things I love about my life

Date: _____

The activities that make me happy:

_____

_____

_____

_____

_____

I will try to do them more often by:

_____

_____

_____

_____

_____

Movies

I AM GRATEFUL FOR:

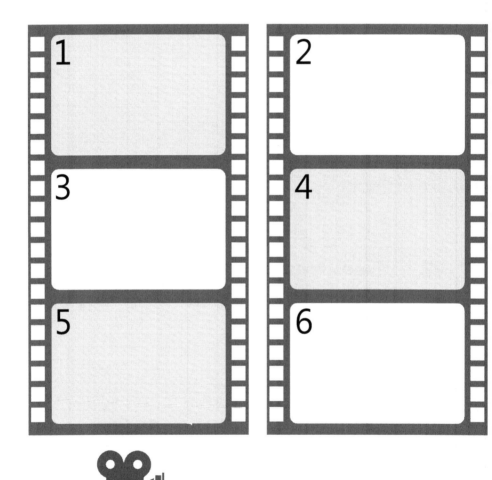

1

2

3

4

5

6

GRATITUDE
Prompts

1. WHO DO YOU LOVE?
2. WHAT MADE YOU SMILE LATELY?
3. WHO DO YOU LIKE?
4. WHAT ARE YOU GOOD AT DOING?
5. WHO CAN YOU COUNT ON?
6. WHAT DO YOU LOVE?
7. WHAT DO YOU LIKE?
8. WHERE DO YOU LIKE TO GO?
9. WHAT DO YOU ENJOY?
10. WHO INSPIRES YOU?
11. LIST ACTIVITIES THAT BRING YOU JOY.
12. LIST ITEMS THAT BRING YOU JOY.
13. LIST PEOPLE THAT BRING YOU JOY.
14. WHAT MAKES YOU HAPPY?
15. WHAT RELAXES YOU?
16. WHAT MAKES YOU SPECIAL?
17. WHAT IS YOUR FAVORITE MEMORY?
18. IS THERE ANYTHING THAT YOU TAKE FOR GRANTED?
19. WHAT IS YOUR FAVORITE FOOD?
20. DESCRIBE ONE GOOD THING THAT
 HAPPENED TO YOU THIS MONTH.

PLACES

I enjoyed visiting:

_____

_____

_____

_____

_____

_____

PEOPLE

I am Grateful For:

_____

_____

_____

_____

_____

_____

_____

GRATEFUL FOR

Monday:

Tuesday:

Wednesday:

Thursday:

Friday:

Saturday:

Sunday:

Thank You

Dear

You don't actually have to send the letter

Things I love
about my life

Date: _____

The activities that make me happy:

_____

_____

_____

_____

_____

I will try to do them more often by:

_____

_____

_____

_____

_____

Movies

I AM GRATEFUL FOR:

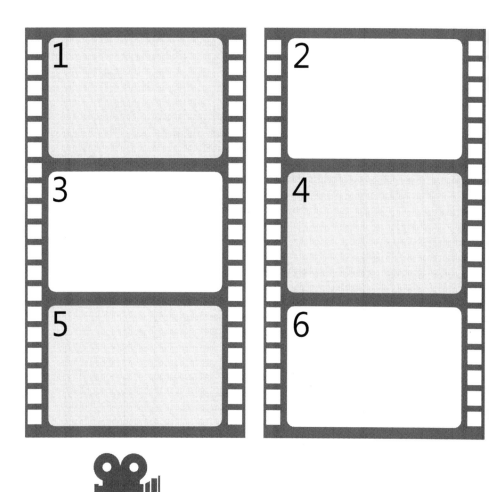

1

2

3

4

5

6

GRATITUDE
Prompts

1. WHO DO YOU LOVE?
2. WHAT MADE YOU SMILE LATELY?
3. WHO DO YOU LIKE?
4. WHAT ARE YOU GOOD AT DOING?
5. WHO CAN YOU COUNT ON?
6. WHAT DO YOU LOVE?
7. WHAT DO YOU LIKE?
8. WHERE DO YOU LIKE TO GO?
9. WHAT DO YOU ENJOY?
10. WHO INSPIRES YOU?
11. LIST ACTIVITIES THAT BRING YOU JOY.
12. LIST ITEMS THAT BRING YOU JOY.
13. LIST PEOPLE THAT BRING YOU JOY.
14. WHAT MAKES YOU HAPPY?
15. WHAT RELAXES YOU?
16. WHAT MAKES YOU SPECIAL?
17. WHAT IS YOUR FAVORITE MEMORY?
18. IS THERE ANYTHING THAT YOU TAKE FOR GRANTED?
19. WHAT IS YOUR FAVORITE FOOD?
20. DESCRIBE ONE GOOD THING THAT
 HAPPENED TO YOU THIS MONTH.

PLACES

I enjoyed visiting:

PEOPLE

I am Grateful For:

_____

_____

_____

_____

_____

_____

_____

GRATEFUL FOR

Monday:

Tuesday:

Wednesday:

Thursday:

Friday:

Saturday:

Sunday:

Thank You

Dear
_____
_____
_____
_____
_____
_____
_____
_____
_____
_____
_____
_____

You don't actually have to send the letter

Made in the USA
Las Vegas, NV
21 February 2022